London's Transport and the Olympics: Preparation, Delivery and Legacy

MALCOLM BATTEN

AMBERLEY

Acknowledgements

Special thanks are due to Jonathan James who was involved in planning rail services during the Olympics for providing much of the text on preparation and services during the Games, for advice, proofreading, and use of his diagrams and photographs.

Thanks to Rodger Green for use of his photograph of the Epping Ongar Railway opening, and to London Borough of Newham archives.

First published 2022

Amberley Publishing
The Hill, Stroud,
Gloucestershire, GL5 4EP

www.amberley-books.com

ISBN: 978 1 3981 1291 9 (print)
ISBN: 978 1 3981 1292 6 (ebook)

British Library Cataloguing in Publication Data.
A catalogue record for this book is available from the British Library.

Typeset in 10pt on 13pt Celeste.
Typesetting by Hurix Digital, India.
Printed in the UK.

Contents

Introduction

When London first applied by the July 2003 deadline as a contender to stage the 2012 Olympic and Paralympic Games, there was cynical speculation as to whether the transport infrastructure could cope should we win. After all, this was Great Britain where public transport was something of a standing joke – think 'the wrong sort of snow', 'leaves on the line', etc. There was also scepticism as to whether we should bid at all. After all, very few other countries had made a profit from staging the Games, and the Olympic venues had often become a white elephant afterwards.

During the bidding process for 2012, Transport for London, the capital's transport strategy provider, did its bit to promote the application with some buses, Tube trains and Stratford station displaying prominent 'Back the Bid' slogans. The first elected London mayor, Labour's Ken Livingstone, was a keen supporter of the bid. In April 2008, during a debate on BBC's *Question Time*, he stated that the primary reason he supported the Olympic bid was to secure funding for the redevelopment of the East End of London. A number of cities were shortlisted to hold the 2012 Olympics and Paralympics, with the final announcement made on 6 July 2005, with London winning over Moscow, New York, Madrid and Paris (who subsequently won the 2024 Olympics). The main stadia and facilities were to be built mostly on redundant railway land around Stratford, predominantly in the London Borough of Newham. The official motto for the Games was 'Inspire a Generation'.

Jubilation turned to horror the next day when terrorists exploded three bombs on the Underground, and another, intended for a Tube train, on a No. 30 bus in Tavistock Square. It all emphasised the massive logistical task ahead facing the authorities in delivering a service during the Olympic and Paralympic Games in just seven years' time. The Games would be reliant on public transport to move the thousands of visitors, officials, VIPs and others, as car parking would be minimal. All this while continuing to run a normal peak-hour service on weekdays through Stratford, one of the busiest interchanges in London. Road traffic would need to contend with such notorious bottlenecks as the Blackwall Tunnel and the City of London, where much of the road layout predates the Great Fire of London.

There was also the question of labour relations. The transport unions, particularly NUR and ASLEF, had a tradition of hard-line opposition to TfL authority. With the purse strings now controlled by a Tory mayor, Boris Johnson, from 2008, and the government imposing a programme of austerity following the financial crisis, the prospect of conflict was ever-present.

Security was another headache, as highlighted by the attacks of 7 July 2005. While we were largely over the Troubles in Northern Ireland, there was the prospect of attacks from militant Islamic extremists and from anarchist groups. Indeed, on 19 July it was revealed that in a six-day period there had been 110 incidents of 'suspect bags' and the like on the Underground, forty-nine of which had caused services to be delayed or suspended. On 21 July three more devices exploded on the Underground and one on a bus – thankfully only one person was injured and there was relatively little damage but considerable disruption.

However, this was not the first time that London had hosted the Olympic Games. It had happened twice in the twentieth century, firstly in 1908 at White City when the Games were originally awarded to Rome, but the eruption of Mount Vesuvius in 1906 meant that funds were diverted to the reconstruction of Naples, so London took over. The second time was in 1948. London had been awarded the Games for 1944, but the war led to its postponement. Because of post-war austerity and a shortage of raw materials, no new venues were built. The Games were centred on Wembley Stadium and participants were housed in schools, government buildings and barracks. Alas, Britain won only three gold medals. So there was a 'can do' mentality amongst transport management on this occasion. The fact that British athletes had done well in the previous two Olympic Games of 2004 and 2008 gave promise that we could achieve a good result in the medal tables on home turf this time, and the public began to get supportive of the Games. This time there would also be the Paralympic Games – an event first held in 1960.

Why was Stratford chosen as the main site? There was a vast acreage of largely redundant railway land. It was a run-down area with declining industries that was seen as in need of regeneration to match the level of regeneration that had already been achieved a few miles south in Docklands. Here the former Royal Docks and West India and Millwall Docks sites had been redeveloped by the London Docklands Development Corporation after closure in the 1980s to recreate a major financial district, a new campus for the University of East London and London City Airport, plus much new housing and jobs.

Living in East London only a few miles from the Olympic site, I travelled through Stratford station daily on my way to and from work, so witnessed the process of construction of the site from start to finish. I also travelled through the Olympic site stations regularly during the Games, experiencing first-hand the general efficiency with which the crowds were handled. When the Olympics and Paralympics took place, the actions of the volunteer champions and guides in making things run smoothly gained particular praise. I have since lived through the aftermath of the Olympics and seen how Stratford and the Olympic site have been transformed subsequently. Although through this period I did not envisage writing this book as such and therefore unfortunately did not photograph the construction, I was photographing the transport scene with a view to writing about the history of buses and railways in East London.

Photographs are by the author except where credited.

Stratford Before the Bid

The first railway lines to serve Stratford were those of the Eastern Counties Railway, whose line opened from Romford to a temporary terminus at Devonshire Street, Mile End, on 20 June 1839. In 1840 this was extended to Shoreditch (later named Bishopsgate), and services reached the City of London at Fenchurch Street station in 1854. The Eastern Counties Railway became a major part of the newly formed Great Eastern Railway in 1862. Stratford became a junction as early as 1840 when the Northern & Eastern Railway line from Broxbourne joined here. Stratford also became the home of the GER's main works and motive power depot. The present London terminus at Liverpool Street station opened in 1874, replacing Bishopsgate.

The Great Eastern Railway, faced with threats from competing trams, had considered electrification in the early twentieth century but were unable to afford the cost. A new proposal to electrify the suburban services from Liverpool Street station over the approximately 20 miles to Shenfield came in 1935 under the New Works Programme, a government series of public investment projects partly to relieve unemployment in the Depression. Major engineering works included the rebuilding of Stratford station and the flyover at Ilford to separate suburban and main line tracks. A new depot was constructed at Ilford to maintain the electric trains.

Another aim of the New Works Programme was to relieve the main line railways of short-distance local traffic which it was thought could be better served by the Underground, now under London Transport ownership. This would also allow the main line companies capacity to develop longer-distance services. Under the same scheme, the route to Epping via Loughton and the Hainault loop were transferred to London Transport to become an extension to the Central line. Work started in the 1930s but was suspended during the war, continuing thereafter to Stratford (1946) and Epping (1949).

Electric services to Shenfield started from 26 September 1949 with a full service in 1950. The original electrification was at 1500 volts DC. Fenchurch Street station was electrified along with the connecting link from Bow Junction with the intention of running a shuttle service between Fenchurch Street and Stratford, but this was dropped as an unnecessary duplication of the new Central line and the new bay platforms 4 and 7 at Stratford were not commissioned.

Electrification was extended to Southend Victoria and also Chelmsford in 1956, also at 1500 volts DC. When the decision was made that all future BR electrification would be on the AC system, all the Liverpool Street DC lines were converted to 25 kV AC in 1959–60 (6.25 kV in the inner-London area), necessitating conversion of the trains to accommodate transformer and rectification equipment.

Electrification was later extended to cover the main lines to Colchester and Clacton in 1962, and to Norwich in 1987. Some of the branch lines which were originally left to DMU operation such as Wickford – Southminster and Witham – Braintree were also electrified and now have direct services from Liverpool Street. The 6.25 kV mileage was converted to 25 kV from 1975 onwards.

In the era of railway privatisation, the local services to East Anglia became the First Great Eastern franchise from January 1997. Until 2004 Liverpool Street was served by three train operating companies – Great Eastern, Anglia, and West Anglia Great Northern – whilst the trains of a two other companies, c2c (ex-LTS Rail), and Silverlink entered at certain times. However, under direction from the Strategic Rail Authority, Liverpool Street station became served by a single 'Greater Anglia' franchise from April 2004. The services operated into there by Anglia, Great Eastern and WAGN were united in a single company owned by National Express trading as One.

Direct links from Stratford to Stansted Airport were also proposed and implemented by the Greater Anglia franchise. Services to Stansted, Hertford East and Cambridge ran from platforms 11 and 12 at Stratford, originally provided for a service to Broxbourne which ran from 1990 to 1992. Stansted Airport had started out as an RAF and US Air Force base in 1943, passing into civilian use in 1949. However, the decision to develop it as London's third airport was not taken until 1979. Expansion then took place with a new terminal and a direct railway branch off the Cambridge line which opened in 1991 and a new 'Stansted Express' service from Liverpool Street calling at Tottenham Hale for the Victoria line. By 2015 the airport would become the third busiest in the UK.

A line ran underneath the main Stratford station serving low-level platforms 1 and 2. Trains ran from North Woolwich to Stratford with some continuing in peak hours to Tottenham Hale via Lea Bridge until this service was withdrawn on 5 July 1985.

In February 1978, BR Chairman Sir Peter Parker announced improvements to the North London line, including investment in the North Woolwich line, and the reopening to passengers of the Stratford–Dalston line with new stations to create a through North Woolwich to Richmond route. Passenger services on this line had been withdrawn in 1944. The Greater London Council would fund this electrification on the basis of the social benefits it would bring to an area needing redevelopment. New stations were built at Dalston Kingsland in 1983 (replacing Dalston Junction), Hackney Central (1980), Hackney Wick (1980) and Homerton (1985).

The initial investment came at West Ham where the line passed underneath the former LTS line and District line tracks right by the station. From 14 May 1979 interchange became possible when a new island platform was opened on the North Woolwich line. A new station was built at North Woolwich alongside the existing 1854 building. Silvertown, Custom House, and Canning Town stations were rebuilt in current BR style.

From 14 May 1979 a thirty-minute-interval DMU service ran Monday–Friday from North Woolwich to Camden Road, supplementing the Broad Street–Richmond service between Canonbury and Camden Road. This was extended to include Saturdays in 1984. This service ended when through electric services commenced between North Woolwich and Richmond from 13 May 1985, marketed as 'North London Link'. This was electrified on the third rail rather than overhead as the existing Broad Street to Richmond services had been electrified this way since 1916.

Following privatisation the line passed to North London Railways, who subsequently rebranded themselves as Silverlink. The Class 313 trains, in use since 1989, were refurbished from 1997 onwards and repainted in the new house colours of purple, green and yellow.

Silvertown station was rebuilt in the late 1980s and renamed Silvertown & London City Airport. It was officially opened by Michael Portillo MP on 7 October 1989.

The London Docklands Development Corporation (LDDC) was set up in 1981 to redevelop the 8 square miles of the London Docks, then in course of closure. This would be achieved by streamlining the planning process for new development and providing a suitable infrastructure, including new transport links. A rail-based system was seen as the key to attracting up to 9,000 jobs to the area. Adopting a light rail system would be cheaper than an extension of the Underground (an option also investigated) and had the advantage of being able to utilise some existing but redundant infrastructure. The original Docklands Light Railway routes were from Tower Gateway to Island Gardens, from where a foot tunnel gives access to Greenwich on the south bank; and from Stratford to Island Gardens, the lines joining at West India Quay. At Stratford the DLR was able to utilise the conveniently vacant bay platform No. 4, originally intended for the shuttle service to Fenchurch Street. The railway was formally opened by HM the Queen on 30 July 1987 and opened to the public a month later. By the time of the bid in 2005 the DLR had had several extensions and new lines – to Beckton, Bank and in November 1999 an extension under the Thames to Lewisham.

A new Stratford station building opened on 14 May 1999, a fitting building for this location's increasingly important role as an interchange. In the same year the station gained yet another new line – the Jubilee Line Extension.

The bill for a 16-km Jubilee Line Extension from Green Park to Stratford via Docklands was deposited in 1989 and gained the royal assent in March 1992. Construction work at the Stratford end started on 29 May 1994. The North London Railways line from Stratford to North Woolwich was closed for a year in order to allow the track to be moved over and the Jubilee line tracks installed between Stratford and Canning Town. The existing stations on the line at West Ham and Canning Town were demolished and new stations built. That at Canning Town also featured platforms for the Docklands Light Railway, which are at an upper level, above the Jubilee line platforms. A new bus station was also provided alongside to create a major new interchange facility, opening in 1999.

At Stratford three terminal platforms were provided alongside the low-level platforms serving the NLR. Rebuilding of the station took place alongside the construction work. A maintenance depot for the Jubilee line trains was built on the site of the former Stratford fruit and vegetable market.

The first section of the Jubilee Line Extension from Stratford to North Greenwich opened to passengers on 14 May 1999. The remainder opened in stages by the end of the year.

The big event of 2000 was to be the Millennium Exhibition at the new Millennium Dome at North Greenwich (since renamed the O2 Arena) on a site adjacent to North Greenwich station. It was anticipated that some 12 million visitors would visit this through the year, with a maximum of around 60,000 on a busy day. These were expected to use public transport as public car parking at the Dome was not provided. There was much political pressure to get the Jubilee Line Extension to Stratford open before the beginning of the year and this was achieved – just! The final cost was almost twice the £1.9 billion anticipated.

The signalling on the Jubilee Line Extension proved to be none too reliable and breakdowns occurred frequently, much to London Underground's and the Department of Transport's embarrassment. To cope with occasions on which the Jubilee line was not functioning a fleet of standby buses was provided, which would only operate when needed, providing a direct link to Canning Town and Stratford stations. The vehicles were all single deck as they would need to run through Blackwall Tunnel. The Millennium Exhibition was not the success that had been anticipated and had to be revamped under new management part-way through the year, but it did give Stratford experience at handling major events.

From 2000 there was a new elected London mayor and a new regulatory authority called Transport for London (TfL) which replaced London Regional Transport. The first London mayor was Ken Livingstone, the former leader of the Greater London Council.

In October 2004 the mayor announced a £10 billion five-year blueprint for public transport including a Thames Gateway Bridge (which didn't happen), and extensions of the DLR to Woolwich Arsenal and from Canning Town to Stratford amongst the plans.

At the beginning of 2005, Stratford was handling some 37,000 passengers in the morning rush hour which was predicted to double in the next ten years.

This aerial view of the Stratford station area dating from 1991 shows the extent of land then occupied by the railway. At the bottom, running from left to right, is the main line and Stratford station, with the low-level tracks to North Woolwich running at right angles below this. North of the station is the Stratford diesel depot and Major Depot repair shops and left of that the London International Freight Terminal. Above is the Freightliner terminal. At the top is Temple Mills Marshalling Yard and the Central line emerges from the tunnel to curve away for Leyton station at the top right corner. (Photo: M. Batten collection)

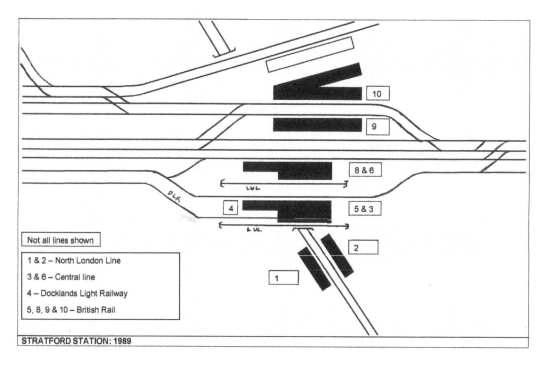

Stratford station layout in 1989. (Diagram by Jonathan James)

An electrically hauled train from Norwich passes Stratford on the through road between platforms 8 and 9 in the late 1980s. The platform buildings seen here would be swept away in the rebuilding. (Photo by Reg Batten)

At the western end of the station, a pair of Class 56 locomotives head a freight train which will turn north onto the North London line link through to Dalston and Willesden. The signal box can be seen above the locomotives. To the left, tracks curve away to reach the depot, carriage sidings, Temple Mills and routes to Harlow, Cambridge, etc. June 1985.

On the same day, a Class 312 EMU runs back to Ilford Depot and passes the signal box on what is now platform 10A. The signal box was also demolished as part of the rebuilding.

A three-car rake of Metro-Cammell DMU stock stands at Stratford Low Level with a train for North Woolwich on 21 July 1969. Services ran from North Woolwich to Stratford with some peak-hour extensions to Tottenham Hale via Lea Bridge until 1979.

The line from Stratford to Dalston reopened to passengers in 1979. A Cravens DMU pauses at Hackney Central on 14 March 1985. This station opened in May 1980. The third rail is in place for the forthcoming electrification which started that May.

Above: The peak-hour-only service from Stratford to Tottenham Hale was withdrawn on 5 July 1985 and the intermediate station at Lea Bridge closed. This was the scene on the morning of the last day.

Right: The North Woolwich line was electrified in May 1985. The original stock used was these Southern Region 2EPB sets. No. 6325 departs Stratford and passes the former Stratford Southern signal box on 14 June 1985.

A variety of diesel locomotives at the 'C' shop of the diesel depot in 1969. 'B' and 'C' shops were completed in 1960. The diesel depot was replaced in July 2001 by a new £11 million EWS facility at Temple Mills as the old depot was due to be swept away when construction started on phase two of the Channel Tunnel Rail Link.

Also in 1969, a Metro-Cammell DMU stands outside the Major Depot repair shops. Diesel multiple units (DMUs) were maintained for lines such as the North Woolwich branch and Romford–Upminster until these lines were electrified and had all gone by the end of 1991.

The repair shops became redundant with electrification of all lines and the privatisation of rail freight haulage and closed in 1991. This line-up of locomotives associated with Stratford was staged to mark the closure. (Photo by Geoff Silcock)

Class 31 No. 31320 departs from the Temple Mills Marshalling Yard with a nuclear flask train for Southminster, the loading point for Bradwell Power Station. The yard was built in the 1950s but the cessation of wagon-load freight made it redundant, and the hump closed in 1982. (Photo by Geoff Silcock)

A Class 08 diesel shunter stands by the Freightliner terminal in February 1979 with the container cranes in the background. As well as this there was the London International Freight Terminal. This was London's first terminal for international rail freight brought in by the train ferries at Harwich and Dover as this was opened in 1967 long before the Channel Tunnel. There were ten sheds used by BR and forwarding agents. Both of these termini had closed by the time of the bid.

The DLR bay platform 4 at Stratford which was originally constructed for a Fenchurch Street shuttle service. An eastbound Central line train is emerging into platform 6. The westbound Central line from platform 3 descends into tunnel to the right of platform 4. 30 December 2000. (Photo by Jonathan James)

A new bus station at Stratford opened on 16 November 1994. The award-winning design replaced a former gloomy and draughty affair below a multistorey car park. This view is from 2005.

A new station building was opened at Stratford in May 1999. This is a surviving part of the former station as seen in 2020. A subway ran underneath the tracks from here which gave staff (and unofficially also trainspotters) access to the depot.

A Jubilee line train at Stratford on the second day of service, 15 May 1999. Three platforms (Nos 13–15) were provided for these services.

For the Millennium Dome events in 2000, a fleet of sixteen standby buses was assembled in case of Jubilee line signal failure. Blue Triangle Leyland Lynx E678 DCU stands at Stratford on 3 February. Behind it is a Dennis Dart of Thorpes, the other partner in the operation. These standby buses were withdrawn officially by 13 October having hardly been used at a time when there was a London wide shortage of bus drivers for regular routes.

The 2EPB sets on the North London line were replaced by Class 313 three-car EMUs in 1989. 313110 stands in the low-level platform with a train for Richmond on 11 June 2002. They were operated by Silverlink as Silverlink Metro.

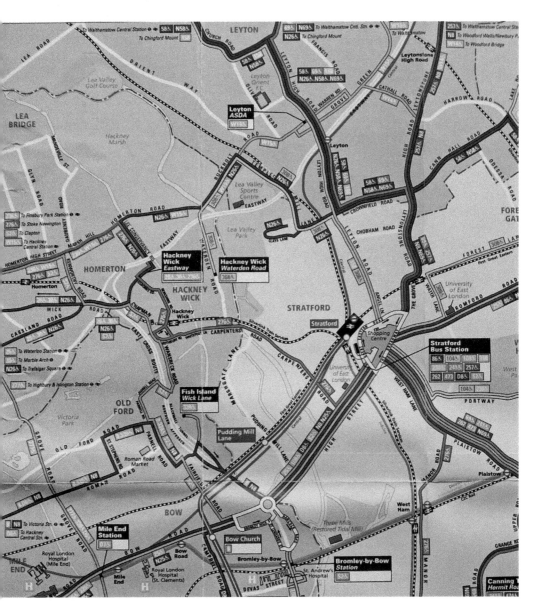

A map showing the rail and bus routes around Stratford as in 2001, from a local Newham Public Transport Guide.

The Bid and Preparation

A cornerstone of the London 2012 Olympics bid was the provision of good-quality public transport, enabling the spectators to use public transport to travel to and from the venues. Of course, a great deal of planning went into the bid, the enhancements to the transport network that followed and execution of the plan during the 2012 Olympics and Paralympics.

A number of organisations were set up to manage the planning and delivery of London 2012, including the London Organising Committee of the Olympic and Paralympic Games (LOCOG), who were responsible for the planning process, and the London Delivery

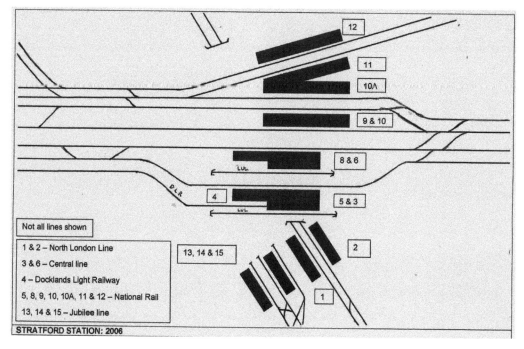

Stratford station layout in 2006. (Diagram by Jonathan James)

Authority (LDA), who were in charge of constructing the Olympic venues. An important element of the bid focussed on sustainability and regeneration of East London, with the London Legacy Development Organisation (LLDO) set up to oversee the longer-term regeneration of the Stratford area, including the Olympic Park (later renamed the Queen Elizabeth Olympic Park). These organisations worked closely alongside the International Olympic Committee (IOC), the Greater London Authority (GLA) and the Olympic Board.

Specific legislation was put in place to give the legal powers necessary to deliver the Games, called the London Olympic Games and Paralympic Games Act. All new rail franchises required operators to produce Olympic Service Delivery Plans.

Furthermore, a major new Westfield shopping centre would be built directly north of Stratford station, on the site of the former Major Depot, with construction work for this going on alongside the transport infrastructure and Olympic venues construction.

Stratford station was given 'Back the Bid' branding as part of the lobbying process to gain support for London's bid to stage the Games. This view was taken on 6 March 2005.

In 2004 forty London buses were given an advertising livery to promote the capital's bid to host the Olympic Games in 2012. Stagecoach No. 18209 was an exhibit at the Showbus rally held at Duxford on 26 September.

The buses were across the range of main companies that now provided London's tendered bus services – Arriva, First, London United, Metroline, Stagecoach and Travel London. Metroline VP569, a 2004 Volvo B7TL with Transbus (Plaxton) body, is seen passing Marble Arch on route 6 on 28 March 2005.

An offside view shows Metroline VP341 in Whitehall on 28 October 2004 while working on route 24. A case of getting the message across to those in power!

Arriva London DW80, a 2004 VDL DB250LF with Wrightbus bodywork, at Hyde Park Corner on 1 April 2005.

The One railway franchise painted Class 315 EMU No. 315812, used on the Liverpool Street–Shenfield local services in a 'Back the Bid' livery and named it 'London Borough of Newham – host borough 2012 Olympic Bid'. The name plaque was unveiled by Newham mayor Sir Robin Wales. The train is seen passing the DLR Pudding Mill Lane station on 31 May 2005.

London Underground treated a Jubilee line train to 'Back the Bid' branding and this is seen at Stratford on 6 December 2004.

The Docklands Light Railway had a pair of two-car sets painted up and lettered for 'Back the Bid'. Car 06 leads in this view near Gallions Reach on 16 January 2005.

Walk the Bid

A Guide to the London 2012 Olympic and Paralympic Games Sites

The cover of a leaflet, 'Walk the Bid', which was produced during the bid period. This included maps of the proposed Olympic Zone and River Zone showing the main event locations and suggesting walks of local interest in these areas. Five London boroughs were included within these zones: Newham, Hackney, Tower Hamlets, and Waltham Forest north of the Thames, Greenwich on the south bank.

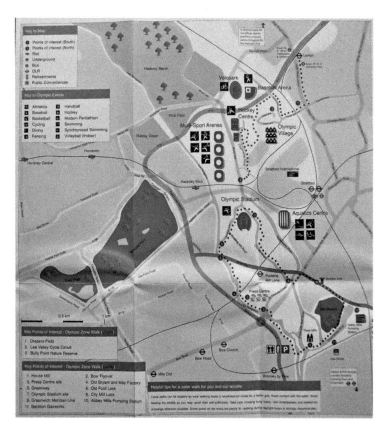

From the 'Walk the Bid' leaflet: a map of the Olympic Zone around Stratford with the proposed Olympic sites and suggested walks, largely using the existing canal paths.

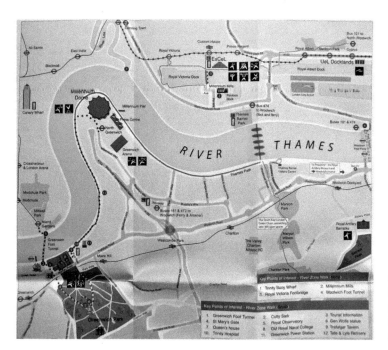

Again from the 'Walk the Bid' leaflet: the map of the River Zone locations and suggested walks.

The Transport Plan

The transport plan took advantage of the various transport schemes already in the planning process or under construction as part of the overall plan. The possibility of completing the Crossrail project in time for the games was briefly explored but discounted (Crossrail aka the Elizabeth line was originally due to open in December 2018 but has been delayed and is now due to open in the first half of 2022). Lessons were also learnt from the Jubilee Line Extension, which was completed shortly before the millennium celebrations in 2000. Although the Jubilee Line Extension was authorised before the 2000 celebrations at the Millennium Dome (now the O2 Arena), the completion of the extension was a critical part of the final plan. Various construction delays put pressure on the Jubilee Line Extension project. The first section to be completed was between Stratford and North Greenwich (for the Millennium Dome) in May 1999, with the remainder of the line opening in September 1999, just over three months before the millennium.

Careful planning was undertaken to make sure that the transport projects promised for London 2012 were completed ahead of time, again with a focus on Stratford and the East End of London.

Whilst the main Olympic venue was at Stratford, a number of other venues around the country were utilised for various events including Hyde Park, Horse Guards Parade and Regent's Park in central London, Wembley Arena, Wimbledon (tennis), Earls Court, Lord's Cricket Ground (archery), Greenwich (equestrian events), Woolwich (shooting) and the Excel Centre in Docklands; also Eton Dorney near Windsor (rowing) and Broxbourne on the lower Lea Valley. In London, it was estimated that 80 per cent of spectators would arrive at Olympic venues by public transport.

Outside of London, sailing took place near Weymouth and Portland on the south coast of England, whilst football stadiums around the country were used for football events.

Various planning meetings were arranged in the run-up to London 2012 to plan the transport service including London Transport, Network Rail and various train operators. Ahead of the games, critical assets were identified and provided with enhanced maintenance, whilst the routine engineering work plan was reviewed to enable additional late-night services to operate during the Olympics and Paralympics.

Modelling was undertaken to establish how long it would take to disperse visitors leaving the Olympic Park, in particular during the evening 'bump out' period, and where people would be travelling to. A number stayed at various hotels and other accommodation around London, whilst others travelled further afield. The last trains from all major London stations were reviewed and where possible additional late-night trains were provided, with routine engineering work times adjusted to facilitate them. Where possible the freight train operators were also encouraged to re-time or divert freight trains away from the Stratford area. Arrangements were made to extend the operation of key Underground lines, with last trains departing central London around an hour later than usual at around 01.30. Underground services also started around an hour earlier on Sundays during the Games.

In addition, analysis was undertaken to establish where spectators would be travelling from, with the highest numbers being 57 per cent from around London, 21 per cent from the South East and 13 per cent from the East of England.

To ensure the smooth transportation of athletes and officials, an Olympic Route Network (ORN) was set up. This consisted of a network of designated roads, linking important locations, including Heathrow Airport, with the venues. Some temporary traffic management arrangements were put in place, including dedicated lanes, temporary closures and re-timing of traffic lights.

The overall transport budget was £886 million, with £429 million allocated to capital projects.

Railways
Summary of Key Rail Schemes

A number of rail schemes were either completed, already in progress or specifically funded for delivery as part of the London 2012 Olympics transport strategy. The main projects in East London are listed below, although there were numerous other smaller projects, station improvements and some temporary facilities constructed as well.

National Rail and London Overground:

- Stratford station capacity improvement works. New platforms 1 and 2 for London Overground. Extension of platform 10a (including Angel Lane loop). Extension of platforms 11 and 12.
- Relocation of Thornton Fields carriage sidings to a new facility at Orient Way, Leyton.
- North London Line Route Improvement Project (NLRIP).
- East London Line extension (Phase 1 from Highbury & Islington to New Cross, Crystal Palace and West Croydon).
- c2c capacity enhancements.
- High Speed 1 (Phase 1 from the Channel Tunnel to Fawkham Junction via Ashford International and Phase 2 from Southfleet Junction to St Pancras International via Ebbsfleet International and Stratford International).

London Underground:

- Central line – New platform 3a at Stratford and an increase to thirty trains per hour in peak times.
- District line – Refurbishment of rolling stock.
- Jubilee line – Trains lengthened to seven carriages. New signalling system to increase capacity.

Docklands Light Railway:

- London City Airport extension (opened December 2005).
- Woolwich Arsenal extension (opened January 2009).
- Stratford International extension.
- Stratford (regional) station new platforms 4a and 4b for Canary Wharf branch.

- Capacity increase across the network to enable three-car trains to operate, including platform extensions and additional trains.
- Station enhancement works, including stations serving Excel.

Stratford Station

Early on in the planning process it was decided that significant investment was required at Stratford station to increase capacity to an estimated 120,000 passengers in the morning peak period. A total of £102.5 million was put aside for enhancements.

This included the extension of platform 10a and the platform line (known as the Angel Lane loop) to enable freight trains to be held in platform 10a clear of Stratford Central Junction. Platforms 11 and 12 at Stratford were also extended.

Following the opening of a new section of the DLR from Canning Town to King George V via London City Airport on 2 December 2005 the Silverlink North London line service was withdrawn between Stratford and North Woolwich in December 2006 as this largely paralleled the route. Services from Richmond and Clapham Junction were diverted to two new platforms at Stratford. These were located alongside platforms 11 and 12 and were numbered 1 and 2 (originally to be called 12a and 12b) and enabled the low-level platforms and the connecting tunnel beneath Stratford station to be used by the DLR (the original platforms 1 and 2 were renumbered 16 and 17).

Other work included the widening of platforms 6 and 8, additional waiting shelters and new or renovated station canopies, a new Northern ticket hall and an improved concourse adjacent to platform 4a and 4b (used by DLR services towards Canary Wharf). The old eastern station subway was reopened, providing three parallel subways beneath the main line platforms.

The westbound Central line (platform 3) was a known bottleneck, so part of the plans involved constructing platform 3a, to provide the westbound Central line with a platform either side of the track.

A new pedestrian footbridge was installed, spanning the whole station complex, to provide access to the new Westfield shopping centre. An extension to the booking area was provided adjacent to this and direct access provided from the station to the bridge.

In a Newham Council newsletter of May 2008, Councillor Connor McAuley the Executive Advisor for Regeneration stated 'Many people will remember the dreary subway used to access the station in days gone by. Since then, the station has transformed immensely

Silverlink Class 313 EMU No. 313104 stands at North Woolwich on 1 May 2006. The line would close on 9 December and this station along with Silvertown & London City Airport would no longer be served by National Rail services.

and will continue to develop to provide the first class facilities residents deserve. At the moment the situation is far from perfect. Passengers are faced with commuter congestion and ticket hall delays. The improvements will help ease this and provide first class facilities and our first visible legacy from the Olympics.'

From February 2008 the Greater Anglia One franchise was rebranded as the more logical National Express East Anglia.

Seen from Platform 12, a Silverlink Class 313 EMU stands 'not in service' at platform 11. The buildings behind would be removed during the rebuilding and the platforms extended. 30 October 2006.

A London Overground Class 313 EMU in Silverlink livery stands in the new platform 2 on 19 April 2009. The new pedestrian bridge across to the Westfield centre is under construction.

Stratford platform changes
From Wednesday 15 April 2009

All London Overground services at Stratford station will run from newly built platforms 1 and 2, located at the far north of the station next to platform 12.

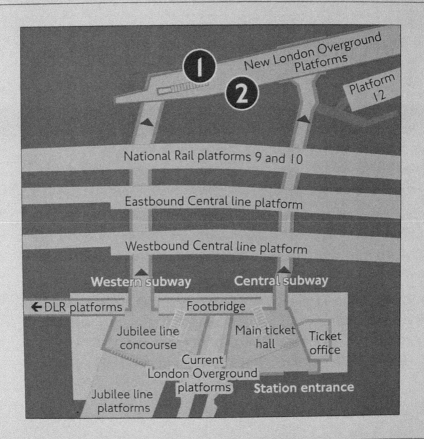

MAYOR OF LONDON

Transport for London

A TfL leaflet advising on the new platforms provided for London Overground services from 15 April 2009.

Stratford station showing the extended booking area and the pedestrian bridge across to Westfield (view from 2020).

Stratford bus station viewed from the steps of the bridge to Westfield. The proximity to the railway station is evident.

London Overground and National Rail Projects

Whilst already in the planning process, the North London Line Route Improvement Project (NLRIP) complemented the overall Olympic plan by providing much-needed additional capacity for both London Overground and freight services across the North London line. The upgrade was part funded from the Olympic budget, with work starting in 2009 and completing in 2011. The work included new track, platform extensions and resignalling, enabling a more frequent London Overground service to be introduced. A £107 million contribution was made by the ODA towards the NLRIP enhancement scheme.

The former North London line services transferred from Silverlink to London Overground in November 2007, moving from Department for Transport (DfT) to Transport for London (TfL) Control. The new concession was awarded to London Overground Rail Operations Limited (LOROL), which was a joint venture between Deutsche Bahn (DB) and the MTR Corporation. A key element of the new concession was successful delivery of the London 2012 Games. In addition to the upgrade to the North London line, a fleet of new Class 378 trains was introduced. These were built by Bombardier in Derby and originally consisted of three-carriage units, which were extended to four carriages in time for the Olympics.

In order to develop the Olympic Park, the Thornton Fields carriage stabling sidings had to be relocated. A site was identified at Orient Way, Leyton, where a fan of new sidings was constructed with a budget of £23 million.

Around £18.5 million was allocated for improvements along the Lea Valley line.

A three-car London Overground Class 378 train at platform 2. Work continues on building the Westfield shopping centre and the access bridge. 13 December 2009.

Stratford International

2 July 2001 saw the end of an era with the closure of Stratford diesel depot, replaced from the same day by a new £11 million EWS diesel servicing facility, retaining the same name but located at Temple Mills. The old depot was due to be swept away as construction started on phase two of the Channel Tunnel Rail Link.

The construction work on the Channel Tunnel Rail Link started almost immediately in July when Transport Minister John Spellar ceremoniously launched a drilling rig to start the building of twin bore tunnels and an international passenger station. This was the culmination of a thirteen-year campaign for a station to be included at Stratford on the high-speed link. The CTRL from St Pancras opened on 14 November 2007, but Stratford International did not open until 30 November 2009.

Above left: Stratford International station with Westfield beyond, seen in 2019. The DLR station is to the right where the van is parked.

Above right: Stratford International is served by Southeastern's high-speed Class 395 trains which run from St Pancras International to various locations in Kent via the HS1 high-speed line. A pair of these are seen just outside Ashford International station.

Left: The Eurostar depot at Temple Mills opened in 2007 replacing a former depot at North Pole, Acton, used when Eurostar services ran from Waterloo.

Docklands Light Railway Projects

The London 2012 budget contributed towards the cost of platform extensions, enabling longer three-unit trains to operate and the Stratford International extension, which opened on 31 August 2011. This included a new entrance at Stratford International station allowing access to the new DLR station and the Olympic Village. Just over £80 million from the ODA budget was allocated to enhancing the DLR ahead of the Olympics.

On the original DLR route platform 4 at Stratford was replaced by new DLR platforms 4A and 4B (although just signposted as '4'). A train is seen in July 2007.

A view looking north from Stratford High Street on 8 June 2009. The Jubilee line platforms are on the left. On the right are the former Silverlink lines from North Woolwich which will become the new DLR line to Stratford International. Westfield shopping centre is under construction in the distance.

Stratford Market station had been built for the original North Woolwich line but had closed in May 1957. It was converted into commercial premises in the late 1960s and saw various uses over the years. In 1994 Newham Council, recognising its historical importance, approved a scheme for its restoration. With the new Stratford extension it reopened as a DLR station. The building itself remains in commercial use – like other DLR stations there is no ticket office. September 2011.

Stratford Low Level. A train is arriving from Stratford International. These platforms are now numbered 16 and 17, the original numbers 1 and 2 being allocated to the new London Overground platforms. 2 October 2011.

The entrance to the DLR platforms at Stratford International is just across the road from the National Rail station.

West Ham station seen in 2001 from what was then the Silverlink North Woolwich line platforms – note the third rail in place.

West Ham station again but with the DLR installed in place of the Silverlink lines. (This view is from 2021.)

A new junction and flyover south of Canning Town station are seen under construction on 31 January 2009. This was to enable trains from either the existing high-level platforms or the low-level platforms on the former Silverlink line from Stratford (then under conversion to DLR) to access either the Beckton or Woolwich Arsenal routes.

By the time of the Games Stratford had the following rail links:

- National Rail services to various locations including London Liverpool Street, Shenfield, Clacton, Southend-on-Sea, Chelmsford, Colchester, Ipswich and Norwich.
- London Overground (North London line) services to Richmond and Clapham Junction via Willesden Junction.
- Southeastern high-speed services at Stratford International to St Pancras and stations in Kent (introduced in 2009).
- Central line services to Ealing Broadway, West Ruislip via central London and towards Epping and the Hainault loop.
- Jubilee line services to central London, Wembley and Stanmore.
- Docklands Light Railway services at Stratford and Stratford International (introduced in 2011).

c2c trains (Fenchurch Street–Southend-on-Sea and Shoeburyness) and London Underground District line and Hammersmith & City line services were also available at nearby West Ham.

Buses

In October 2007 the Olympic Delivery Authority made a presentation about transport needs for the Games. They stated that four separate bus or coach transport systems would be required for athletes, officials, the media and spectators. They estimated some 400 buses and 1,100 coaches would be needed plus cars and minibuses and that consultation on vehicle specifications, service levels and a procurement strategy should begin by summer 2008.These services would need to start before the actual Games commenced because of the set-up period. There would be special 'express bus lanes'. For spectators, there would be no car parking at the Olympic Park but purchasers of a ticket for an Olympic event would get a free one-day Travelcard.

On 9 April 2008 the ODA awarded a four-year contract to transport workers within the Olympic Park complex to a combination of Ealing and Hackney Community Transports using hired vehicles from Dawson Rentals.

In June 2009 the ODA published revised figures. LOCOG would contract the vehicles for athletes, officials, sponsors and the media and an estimate of 1,800 buses, minibuses and coaches was quoted. The ODA would provide park-and-ride services for spectators at various venues – some 600 vehicles and tender out express coach services direct to the Olympic Park. The ODA contract was later awarded to First Group. First Group announced plans to order 460 buses for 2011/2 and 495 buses for 2012/3 which would include vehicles first earmarked for use at the Olympics.

In February 2011 the ODA announced that TfL would take responsibility for Games Travel Demand Management and the route networks. Three temporary depots were planned for the vehicles – next to West Ham bus garage (athletes transport), Royals Business Park (officials and judges) and Millennium Mills (media).

By March 2011 LOCOG appointed operators for its share of operations. A revised total of 1,250 vehicles from forty-four operators all over the United Kingdom would be used. These included major operators like Abelio, Arriva, Go-Ahead, and Stagecoach as well as various smaller companies. Stagecoach ordered 390 new buses for 2012 for their non-London operations, some of which would first be used for the Games.

There were some significant changes in the ownership of the companies who ran tendered services on behalf of TfL in the years before 2012. Stagecoach sold their London operations to Australian investment company Macquarie Bank in August 2006 for £263.5 million. The new owners were known as the East London Bus Group and reused the former fleetnames of East London and Selkent (south of the Thames). In 2010 the business was put up for sale and eventually after speculation that it might go to French company RATP it was bought back by Stagecoach in October for a cut-price £52.8 million.

While three of the main players (Arriva, First and Stagecoach) already had a presence in East London, the fourth, Go-Ahead, did not, but this soon changed when they bought out two of the smaller companies with tendered routes in the area.

East Thames Buses, originally set up by TfL following the collapse of Harris Bus, was sold to Go-Ahead London General in 2009. Arriva was bought by Deutsche Bahn in 2010, although the Arriva name was retained.

The new Westfield Stratford City development opened on Tuesday 13 September 2011 and a new Stratford City bus station was provided adjacent to this. Initially four routes were diverted or extended to serve this: the 97, 241, 339 and D8. The 97 (now Chingford–Stratford City) also gained a frequency increase.

To replace Trident No. 17758, which was destroyed in the 7 July 2005 bombing at Tavistock Square, Stagecoach received No. 18500. This was the first bus to the new design of Alexander Dennis Enviro400 body and was named *Spirit of London* to honour the dead and injured of the bombing. Initially normally working on route 30, it sometimes strayed on to other routes, but is seen here at the Cobham Gathering, held at Wisley Airfield on 2 April 2006.

On 18 September 2006 Go-Ahead paid £3 million cash to buy Docklands Minibuses, who were operating three routes from a base in Silvertown with around thirty Dennis Darts, plus another route due to start in November that year (the W19). This gave Go-Ahead a presence and base in East London for the first time, and thus an opportunity to bid for contracts arising with the upcoming Olympic Games in 2012. The most recent vehicles in the Docklands Buses fleet were Dennis Darts with MCV Evolution bodywork such as AE06 HCC seen in Barking on 16 April.

On 29 June 2007 the Go-Ahead Group announced that they had expanded their presence in East London by paying £12 million cash for Blue Triangle Buses and its local bus operations. The deal included sixty-eight buses, the Rainham depot, eight TfL contracts, nine Essex contracts and rail replacement work. Like the Docklands company bought earlier, the name would be kept and the business run as an autonomous unit within Go-Ahead London. Representing the bus fleet at the time is TL901, a 1999-built Dennis Trident with East Lancs bodywork at North Woolwich on 10 December 2006.

The two East London Bus Company garages in Waterden Road, Stratford, were scheduled for closure as they came within the area that would be redeveloped as the Olympic Games site. A new site was found by the Olympic Delivery Authority near West Ham station on land used formerly by Parcelforce, although the Mercedes artics for route 25 initially moved temporally to Rainham. A farewell open day was held at Waterden Road on 16 February 2008 at which RML 2760 and T1, both part of the heritage fleet, are seen together. First Capital's garage, also in Waterden Road, was replaced by the new Lea Interchange site at Temple Mills Lane, Leyton.

Also present at Waterden Road was No. 18500 *Spirit of London*. Note how the livery has been changed since 2006.

The road closures associated with the creation of the Olympic Games site led to the re-routing of some bus routes that previously traversed these roads. One such route was the 276 (Newham Hospital–Stoke Newington) which from July 2008 was routed via Bow instead of via Carpenters Road, Stratford. Seen in Stratford in July 2009 is one of East London's first hybrid-powered vehicles, Optare Tempo No. 29005.

The new Stratford International station on the HS1 high-speed line from St Pancras International opened on 30 November 2009. Because the station was within the building site for the London Olympics development and Westfield shopping centre there was no public access, so a bus shuttle was provided from Stratford station. Go-Ahead won the contract and bought eight Dennis Dart SLFs from Metroline for the service, such as R147 RLY seen here. The extension of the DLR from Stratford to Stratford International (opening in August 2011) eventually did away with the need for this.

The Go-Ahead Group won a contract to operate a frequent shuttle service between Stratford and the Athletes' Village on behalf of the ODA from 13 September 2010. This Volvo PVL258 was at Stratford station working the shuttle on 3 September 2011. This contract ceased on 17 September 2011 following the opening of the DLR extension to Stratford International.

Labour Relations and the Trade Unions

In the years leading up to the Games the RMT Trade Union called a Tube strike from 19.00 on Tuesday 9 June 2009 to the end of service on 11 June. There were further Tube strikes on 7 September and 29 November 2010. Pay deals reached for train workers with London Overground, Network Rail and the DLR included bonuses of from £500 to £900 for the Games period. London Underground also negotiated a deal. The Unite union then called on the mayor for a similar deal for bus drivers but were initially told that this was a matter for the separate bus operators. The mayor stated that he had obtained £8.3 million from the ODA for a bonus of £500 to be paid to employees at any garage where one or more routes was affected by the Games. This was rejected and a strike ballot voted in favour of strike action. A one-day strike was held on 22 June 2012 affecting most operators and Unite called for two more strikes on 5 and 24 July. A deal was eventually agreed which would give all staff a payment of £27.50 per duty over the twenty-nine days of the Games. With an average of twenty-one duties each this amounted to around £577. The strike planned for 24 July was called off.

River Transport

The Olympic Delivery Authority had a target of transporting 50 per cent of construction materials by sustainable means. With a number of rivers, known as the Bow Back Rivers, running through the Olympic site, British Waterways came up with a scheme to allow these to be used. A new lock and sluice on the Prescott Channel near Three Mills was constructed to allow navigation at all times. The lock is 62 m by 8 m, allowing access by 350-ton barges. It was anticipated that up to 1.75 million tons of construction materials could be moved upriver from wharves on the Thames, saving the equivalent of 1,200 lorry journeys. The £23 million project was funded by British Waterways, the Department for Transport, London Thames Gateway Development Corporation, the ODA and TfL. City Mills Lock was also refurbished at a cost of £400,000. In practice very little construction material used the river.

Three Mills Lock on the Prescott Channel opened in June 2009. There had been a lock here previously but this had been removed in the 1980s after falling into disuse, leaving this channel tidal. The new lock was constructed to restore navigation at all phases of the tide and allow construction materials for the London Olympics site to be moved by barge.

A Steam Railway for North Woolwich?

The tourism and hospitality industries naturally expected to benefit from the Games being hosted in London. London's tourist attractions also expected a higher footfall with the large number of visitors coming to the capital.

In the August 2006 issue of *Steam Railway* magazine there was a very interesting feature on the proposals by the London Rail Heritage Centre group to create a steam railway on the then soon to be redundant North Woolwich line between the North Woolwich Old Station Museum and Custom House.

The museum had opened in 1984 after the old Grade II listed North Woolwich station was replaced by a new station alongside in 1979. Open daily, it had a restored booking office and displays relating to the history of the Great Eastern Railway.

As was mentioned in the magazine, when the museum originally opened there were ambitious plans to have a working steam railway. This would have run alongside the British Rail line as far as Silvertown, utilising the spare track where the line had been singled. The plan was to make use of the old goods yard area for a locoshed/large exhibits building. It was intended to eventually run two preserved locomotives, 'Merchant Navy' No. 35010 *Blue Star* and 'Black Five' No. 45293, when they had been restored. At the time these were stored in a warehouse in the old disused docks, but both later moved on for restoration at the Colne Valley Railway. The museum did have a working Peckett 0-6-0ST, No. 2000, for some years, but it never got any further than steaming the length of the platform, and later left the site. As with many proposals it was all too ambitious and there wasn't the money forthcoming. The museum settled down to a static existence and gradual deterioration.

After closure of the North Woolwich line, the section of track between Canning Town and North Woolwich would be mothballed as part of the trackbed would be utilised by Crossrail when it was constructed. But as work on Crossrail was not expected to begin until 2013, in the meantime the section from North Woolwich to Custom House would be made available to the London Rail Heritage Centre for a temporary steam railway operation. This could start operation as early as June 2007 but would cease after 2012 once Crossrail construction was due to commence. The existing museum would be expanded into the vacant former goods yard where new locomotive and carriage sheds would be built. Also, in the yard area would be established 'Railschool' – a training centre teaching NVQ training modules for students aged fourteen to nineteen planning to enter the railway industry.

LRHC were planning to bring in former GWR pannier tank No. 7752 to work the line. This would be overhauled at its home base of Tyseley and repainted to its latter guise as London Transport L94, as which it was the last steam loco to operate for London Transport. It would be supplemented by an 'Austerity' 0-6-0ST from Tyseley, which would be painted in the blue livery of the Port of London Authority who operated similar engines. As the line would not operate all year round, the locos would return to Tyseley in winter for any heavy maintenance required.

Future plans for 2008–09 included returning North Woolwich station to its 1938 condition. The roof design was modified after wartime damage. A turntable would be refitted in the pit. This could lead to the disposal elsewhere of the one steam locomotive then currently at the museum – the former GER 'Coffee Pot' Y5 0-4-0ST No. 229 located in the turntable pit. The museum collection would be expanded to become a museum of London's suburban railways.

Another option being considered was to retain the third rail electrification so that preserved EMUs could also operate, although this was not seen as a high priority.

The whole scheme would be funded by private-public partnership, with some of the funding already secured. The peak year of operation would be 2012, when the railway would benefit from the massive influx of visitors for the Olympic Games being staged at Stratford. Meanwhile tourism packages with other local attractions were planned, and Custom House already attracted thousands of visitors as it was the station for the Excel exhibition centre – home of the London Boat Show, Motor Show, etc. Newham were certainly keen to capitalise on its once in a lifetime opportunity to put itself 'on the map' with the Olympics. With the political will in place, the track in place, and stock plans sorted out, there remained the crucial matter of granting the necessary licences and raising the funds.

Alas, it was not to be. The area was not in a tourist location, so visitor numbers would be likely to be lower than in the Olympic year. The museum's owners, the London Borough of Newham, were facing spending cuts like all local authorities and the museum was not seen as a priority. The site was run-down, stripped of its dedicated curators and reduced to only being open on Saturday and Sunday afternoons from 13.00 to 17.00.

2008 saw a further downturn in the museum's fortunes. The former GER 'Coffee Pot' Y5 0-4-0ST No. 229 was removed ahead of new building work starting alongside the station and returned to its owner's premises. Then many of the other exhibits were removed, several going to the East Anglian Railway Museum at Chappel & Wakes Colne. Then finally in December the London Borough of Newham decided to close the museum and hand the site back to the landlord. An officer's report to the council said, 'It has not proved possible to find a partner to develop the museum into a visitor attraction and education venue.'

The exterior of the GER North Woolwich station when it was in use as a museum.

A platform view of the museum. The Silverlink platform is in the foreground with part of the 1979 station building just visible to the right of the lamp post. The GER 'Coffee Pot' Y5 0-4-0ST No. 229 located in the turntable pit and the museum platform, from which the projected steam service would have run, is to the left of the fence.

Here is one steam locomotive that did make an appearance, although in a more static mode! *Robert* is a 1933-build Avonside 0-6-0ST which worked at an ironstone mine in Northamptonshire. It was bought by the LDDC and originally displayed at the site of Beckton Gas Works. It passed to the London Borough of Newham in 2000 and moved to Stratford until 2008. It was then taken to the East Anglian Railway Museum while construction work for the Olympics took place at Stratford, returning newly repainted to its present plinth outside the station in 2011.

Delivery During the Games

The London 2012 Games were held between 28 July and 12 August, with the opening ceremony taking place on 27 July. In advance of this the Media Centre opened on 27 June and the Olympic Village opened on 15 July.

The London 2012 Paralympic Games were held between 30 August and 9 September, with the opening ceremony taking place on 29 August.

The various venues were divided into Zones: the Olympic Park, the River Zone (including Excel, Greenwich and Woolwich), the Central Zone (including Earls Court, Horse Guards Parade, Hyde Park, Lord's and Regent's Park), Other Venues (Including Broxbourne, Eton Dorney, Weald County Park, Weymouth & Portland and Wimbledon) and finally the various football stadiums used around the country.

Accommodation was provided for athletes and team officials at the Olympic Village in Stratford, the Royal Holloway College (near Eton Dorney) and in Portland Harbour (for sailing).

The Games Transport Co-ordination Centre (TCC) was set up at the TfL offices called Palestra House (opposite Southwark Underground station), to manage the transport delivery, working closely with all transport providers and the London Traffic Control Centre (LTCC).

There were three main client groups to be transported:

- The 'Games Family' of athletes, team officials, supporting organisations and media. This was around 77,000 people of whom around 55,000 would be in the UK at any one time.
- Ticketed spectators. Up to 180,000 spectators a day entered the Olympic Park, the principal area of activity.
- More than 140,000 site workers, including 70,000 volunteers.

An advantage of the Games being held at this time was no school traffic as schools were on holiday, and commuter traffic would also be reduced by around one fifth through holidays.

A number of 'test' events were held in the run-up to the Games themselves, to assess not just the venues but also fine-tune the public transport provision. One of these was on Woolwich Common between 15 April and 7 May. Other cultural events took place during the Games period, including the Notting Hill Carnival in west London, which took place on the 26 and 27 August. HM the Queen's Diamond Jubilee was also celebrated in June.

Railways
Olympic Park Zone Travel

Passengers travelling to and from the Olympic Park at Stratford were encouraged to use four stations: Stratford (regional), Stratford International, Hackney Wick and West Ham. The walking route from West Ham to the Olympic Park was upgraded and clearly signposted. In order to manage passenger flows during the games themselves, the decision was made to close Hackney Wick in the westbound direction and Pudding Mill Lane DLR station which only had a narrow island platform closed completely.

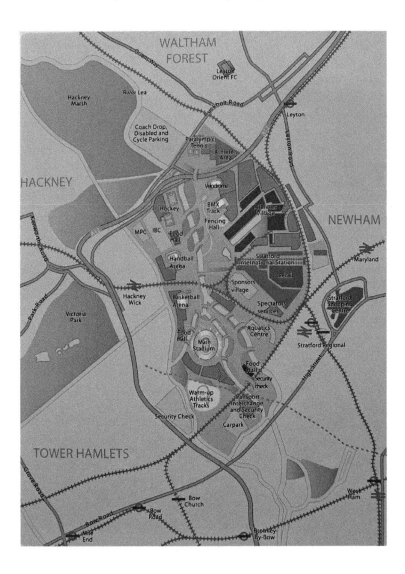

The final layout of the Olympic Park and its rail connections, as published in a Newham Council newsletter. Note that Pudding Mill Lane station is not shown as this was closed during the Games period.

The Javelin service was the linchpin of the London 2012 transport plan. The fleet of Class 395 Hitachi units built for Southeastern trains for services on High Speed 1 and services through Kent were used to provide a high-speed and high-frequency service between St Pancras International, Stratford International and Ebbsfleet International. These units were introduced in 2009, so by 2012 were operating very reliably and providing services to various locations on and off High Speed 1. The Javelin brand was introduced for the Olympics but has subsequently been used to describe Southeastern high-speed services. During the Olympics and Paralympics the Southeastern high-speed services was reduced on some routes to enable the twenty-nine six-car units to be utilised on the Javelin shuttle, often operating as twelve-carriage sets.

At St Pancras International, Stratford International and Ebbsfleet International additional signage and staff were provided and one-way systems installed, along with queuing arrangements, to make sure that there was a safe flow of passengers through the stations. There was a special focus on the 'bump out' times when major events finished at the various venues around the Olympic Park, resulting in an increased flow of passengers.

Ebbsfleet International is located alongside the A2 and is only 5 miles from the M25 London orbital motorway. Road passengers were encouraged to drive to Ebbsfleet International and then join the Javelin service for the ten–twelve-minute journey to Stratford International. The station was equipped with several large car parks (up to 9,000 vehicles) for both commuters and international travellers. The independent bus operator Go Coach were engaged to provide a shuttle service from car park D (the furthest from the station) and the station building.

At St Pancras International and Ebbsfleet International the Javelin service used the usual Southeastern platforms. However, at Stratford International all four platforms were needed for the Javelin service, including the outer two platforms (1 and 4) which were built for Eurostar Class 373 using the Continental loading gauge. These platforms were too low for use by the Class 395 units, so a temporary platform surface was installed to increase the height of the platforms allowing safe and level access to and from the Class 395 units. This did not create any issues for Eurostar and their trains did not serve Stratford International.

During most of the day, eight services per hour operated in each direction between St Pancras international and Ebbsfleet International, one of which was extended to and from Faversham (which resulted in a reduced service for passengers on this route) and two of which operated to and from Ashford International. A number of additional peak-hour services were also withdrawn. The remainder of the services reversed at Ebbsfleet International. Between 23.00 and 01.00 the frequency increased to twelve trains per hour to accommodate the evening 'bump out' period.

Overnight, a half-hourly shuttle service was provided between St Pancras and Stratford International.

The journey time was seven minutes from St Pancras International to Stratford International and a further ten minutes from Stratford International to Ebbsfleet International. The Javelin service carried 15 per cent of visitors to the Olympic Park, with 1.4 million journeys during the Olympics, averaging 90,000 passengers per day, with the peak day being the 6 August, when 131,000 passengers were carried.

A Southeastern Class 395 Javelin train calling at the Eurostar platforms at Stratford International during the Games. The platforms were built to the Eurostar loading gauge, so had to have a temporary raised surface installed to meet the Class 395 loading gauge. They usually use island platform 2/3. (Photo by Jonathan James)

Southeastern passenger numbers increased by around 20 per cent during the Olympics, with 7.7 million additional passengers carried on Javelin and domestic services and a PPM of 96 per cent achieved overall. PPM is the public performance measure, which is based on the number of trains arriving within five minutes of the correct time (ten minutes for InterCity journeys).

c2c Services

The c2c services between Fenchurch Street, Southend-on-Sea and Shoeburyness were expected to be very busy during the Games. A joint control centre was established at Upminster Signalling Centre with Network Rail to co-ordinate operations. A number of additional shuttle services were operated between Fenchurch Street and Barking via West Ham. c2c passengers increased by 31 per cent during the games.

West Ham

West Ham station was also upgraded ahead of the Olympics to provide additional capacity. West Ham was one of the Olympic Park 'gateway' stations, with an enhanced walking route (Greenway) provided between West Ham and Stratford in addition to the DLR and Jubilee line connections. The walking time from West Ham to the Olympic Park south entrance was around twenty–twenty-five minutes.

Greater Anglia

Additional stops were introduced at Stratford (regional) station, facilitated by the major works that took place ahead of the Olympics, including the extended platform 10a. Greater Anglia passengers increased by 19 per cent during the Games.

Enhancements were made at other stations located close to the Olympic venues. Cheshunt station was equipped with a temporary entrance from platform 1 (the main London-bound platform) to provide access to the canoe and kayak venue located in the Lea Valley Country Park. This consisted of a gate and ramp leading down to the footpaths leading to the venue and was removed after the event.

London Overground (North London Line)

The London Overground service ran at an increased frequency, utilising the additional capacity provided by the NLRIP scheme and aided by a number of freight services being diverted via alternative routes.

Docklands Light Railway (DLR)

During the Olympics the DLR carried over 7 million passengers, which was around double normal traffic levels.

London Underground

The Olympic torch was carried by a District line train on the 24 July between Wimbledon and Wimbledon Park. The D Stock unit had special Olympic signage fitted.

The Underground network saw an increase in traffic of around 30 per cent during the Olympics, with around 60 million Tube journeys made during the Olympics. The busiest day was 7 August when 4.5 million journeys were made – a Tube record.

The Underground network ran more late-night trains, with services finishing around an hour later and starting an hour earlier on Sunday mornings during the games. The only significant issue was a signal failure affecting the Central line on the first day of the games, but the contingency plans worked well, with only minimal disruption.

River Zone Travel (including Excel, North Greenwich, Greenwich and Woolwich)

The main routes and stations were:

Docklands Light Railway – to Royal Victoria and Custom House for Excel, Woolwich Arsenal, Greenwich and Cutty Sark.

Jubilee line – to North Greenwich.

Southeastern (National Rail) – to Greenwich, Maze Hill, Woolwich Arsenal, Woolwich Dockyard.

Emirates Air Line (cable car) – between North Greenwich and Royal Docks.

Right: The controversial Emirates Air Line cable car opened on 28 June 2012. This runs across the Thames between Greenwich Peninsula (near the O2) and Emirates Royal Docks (near the Excel Centre). This view from 2012 shows the towers across the Thames from the Greenwich side.

Below: The Emirates Royal Docks terminal which is close to the Excel Centre, the site for martial arts, weightlifting and table tennis. The Emirates Air Line was seen by many as a vanity project by the mayor rather than a vital part of the transport infrastructure.

Central Zone Venues

The Central Zone, which included Earls Court, House Guards Parade, Hyde Park, Lord's cricket ground and Regent's Park was served by numerous Underground lines as well as national rail at London termini such as Marylebone (Chiltern line).

Other London Area Venues

Other venues in the London area included Wembley Stadium, served by LUL Metropolitan and Jubilee lines to Wembley Park, Bakerloo line and London Overground to Wembley Central, and Chiltern line to Wembley Stadium stations. Tennis was played at Wimbledon, served by the District line to Wimbledon and Southfields, South West Trains to Wimbledon, and also the Croydon Tramlink to Wimbledon.

Marylebone station had been proposed for closure in the early 1980s, but privatisation as Chiltern line has seen major investment and expansion of services. Chiltern line services were convenient for Central Zone venues, particularly the nearby Lord's cricket ground and also Wembley Stadium for football.

Contingency Plans

All of the rail operators developed detailed contingency plans. Some flexibility was built into the timetables to allow for events over-running at the Olympic Park or to mitigate disruption on adjacent rail and bus routes.

The Southeastern Javelin timetable was designed with some flexibility, enabling additional trains to operate if required.

London Overground received some additional Class 378 units in readiness for the East London line extension to Clapham Junction (which opened in December 2012) and these were put on standby during the Games (referred to as 'hot spares') to provide additional services if required or replace any defective rolling stock.

c2c also had some 'hot spares' located at East Ham Depot.

In addition, DB Shenker (now DB Cargo) were contracted to have six rakes of Riviera coaches (along with a Class 67 or Class 90 locomotive) on standby at Wembley to operate additional Inter-City services from Kings Cross, Euston, St Pancras or Paddington if required. In the event, the only additional trains required were between Cardiff and Paddington via Bristol Temple Meads after the football in Cardiff.

A number of 'Thunderbird' locomotives were placed on standby at various strategic locations around London to assist with any failed freight or passenger trains if required.

Buses
Special Services

Special services were operated for the 'Games Family' – athletes, media, sponsors, etc., on behalf of the London Organising Committee for the Olympic Games (LOCOG) who banned operator names and advertising from appearing on these vehicles, basically to protect sponsorship deals. Blind displays were set to blank. Some vehicles also had the maker's name, e.g. Scania, removed. Most were new vehicles that were awaiting entry to service with their companies. Stagecoach (Stagecoach UK Bus Events Ltd) was the lead operator contributing around 500 vehicles out of the total of 1,000 plus, none of these coming from their London fleet. Vehicles were stabled at West Ham and at Beckton Park in the Royal Docks.

The park-and-ride services operated by First (First Games Transport Ltd) were numbered and operated non-stop on variable dates as required. This also included routes to sites such as Lea Valley White Water Centre and Eton Dorney near Windsor. Some 200 buses were in use overall.

First also operated express services from the Hertfordshire Showground at Redbourn to Stratford.

Fewer vehicles were required for the Paralympics, so many of the buses had departed by then. But those single-deckers that were retained for athletes' transport needed to be adapted to carry wheelchairs. This was done during the period between the two sets of Games, and of course all the seats removed had to be put back afterwards. The last bus finally departed back home on 27 September.

The main centre for Olympic bus operations was the Eton Manor Transport Hub, next to the New Spitalfields Market which had been relocated to here in 1991. This was on the north side of the Olympic site. On 5 August three buses wait for the traffic lights to enter the site, the two nearest vehicles hailing from Translink Ulsterbus in Northern Ireland.

Another of the fifty-six Translink Volvo/Wright double-deck buses at Eton Manor on 4 August. Vehicles carried stickers with their duty details on their windscreens.

Translink also provided several coaches of two types. This is 1001, an Irizar-bodied Scania.

The other Translink coach type is represented by 1772, a Volvo with Sunsundegui bodywork.

Stagecoach were the leading provider on the Olympics services. This Alexander Dennis E400 from the Manchester fleet leads a convoy departing from the Eton Manor Transport Hub on 4 August.

Although the operator names were not displayed, many of the vehicles provided carried dedicated route branding. Stagecoach ADL Enviro300 27671 carries 'Pulse' branding for local routes around Worthing, Sussex.

Stagecoach 27697 carries branding for route X24 Blaenavon–Newport in South Wales. It is followed by Arriva London DW123, a VDL DB250LF with Wright bodywork.

More route branding on E300 27739 at North Greenwich on 5 August. The O2 Arena was renamed North Greenwich Arena for the duration as O2 were not Games sponsors (but Vodaphone were).

While most Stagecoach vehicles were easily recognisable from their corporate colours, less obvious was 19570 which carries a dedicated livery for Park & Ride services in Exeter.

Another variation on Stagecoach livery was this red-based scheme used on vehicles that serve the University of Warwick, photographed on 27 July near Canning Town.

A National Express West Midlands Alexander Dennis E40D in the light blue colour for Coventry services precedes an Arriva vehicle in corporate livery on 6 August.

Intended for Go-Ahead fleet Wilts & Dorset at Bournemouth was this Wright-bodied Volvo B7RLE, one of nine provided. Note the boundary sign showing that the bus is just leaving the London Borough of Waltham Forest.

Thamesdown Transport (Swindon) were the owners of this Wright Streetlite single-decker. The Eton Manor Transport Hub can be seen to the left.

There were also buses from independent companies, such as this Alexander Dennis E400 for Stephensons of Rochford, Essex.

Making a change from the usual Alexander Dennis or Volvo chassis is this Mercedes-Benz Citaro of Universitybus, Hatfield. As the university was on vacation, these were not needed for normal service.

While buses predominated, there were also coaches. We have already seen examples from Ulsterbus. This Plaxton-bodied coach was from Logan, Dunloy, Northern Ireland.

While most of the vehicles employed were new or recent deliveries, there were some older buses as well. Metroline's VPL630, a Volvo B7TL, dated from 2005 – seen on 4 August.

The oldest bus I photographed was KV02 URX, a 2002 built Dennis Trident/TransBus ALX400 formerly TA83 in the fleet of Abellio London. It was one of a batch 9773–94 which were painted white and allocated to LOCOG for this work.

Two cruise ships, the *Braemar* of Fred Olsen Line and *Gemini* of Gemini Line, were moored in Royal Albert Dock to provide accommodation for the hundreds of bus drivers brought in from all over the country to drive the 'Games Family' – athletes, media, sponsors, etc. – between venues. This view was taken from the Docklands Light Railway on 15 July and shows the two vessels along with many of the buses parked up on the quayside. These ships departed after 12 August. Other accommodation was provided at the nearby University of East London.

First Bus won the contract for spectator Park & Ride services for which there was no fleetname ban. Volvo B9TL 36244 heads along Silvertown Way running to the Excel Arena from Canning Town. This route 21 ran from 28 July to 12 August, every three minutes from 06.00 to 20.20. 28 July.

Route 22 linked North Greenwich with Charlton station, on which another Volvo is seen at North Greenwich with the O2 Arena in the background. This ran between the same dates, frequency as required.

At least five of First's Volvos are seen laying over at North Greenwich. Volvos 36244–80 were based at Barking for these services and Park & Rides from Thurrock Lakeside to London. Most of these subsequently went to First West Yorkshire. Twenty Volvo B9TLs from Ulsterbus were also provided as a 'contingency' but these saw little use.

Some temporary changes were made to bus routes and service frequencies in addition to changes to some bus stops along the Olympic Road Network (ORN) and Paralympics Road Network (PRN). In the run-up to the Olympics some new, greener buses were introduced and work took place to enhance bus information systems. A number of road events took place during the Olympics (cycling and the marathon for example), which required temporary changes to bus routes. Stratford City bus station was closed 'for security' from 6 June with the routes serving it – 97,241,339 and D8 diverted to the main Stratford bus station. Existing night bus services were enhanced and route 238 (Stratford–Barking) gained a night service. Night services reached a peak allocation of 944 buses for Saturday nights during the Olympics as opposed to 888 beforehand.

On 27 July the Olympic torch was carried along Oxford Street on open-top Routemaster RMC1510.

London bus routes 308 and D8 were converted to double-deck for the period to cope with expected extra Olympic traffic as they passed Games sites. First London VNW32353 on the 308 approaches the entrance to the Eton Manor Transport Hub on 12 August.

Route 129 serving North Greenwich received double-deck buses during the period. Another local route, the 132, received some double-deckers during the Olympics to release extra single-deckers for the 108. Go-Ahead's PVL355 departs North Greenwich with an extra on route 132 displaying makeshift blinds on 5 August. During the Paralympics the whole route was worked with new double-deck buses.

On the same day Go-Ahead London Central's PVL90 works an extra service on route 108. Route 108 runs from Stratford to Lewisham via the Blackwall Tunnel, but as the tunnel can only take single-deck vehicles, the extra double-deck buses only ran from North Greenwich to Lewisham.

With the eyes of the world on London during 2012 and thousands of extra visitors coming to the capital, many companies were prepared to pay for advertising on London buses and TfL was only too willing to take their cash. The largest advertising contracts were from companies who were also sponsoring the Olympics. Visa had fifty buses with this advert featuring Usain Bolt (who was to achieve double gold success). First Bus had received a large fleet of Wright-bodied Volvos in 2011 for routes 25 and 58 and VN36126 is seen in Ilford on a route that passes through Stratford.

Samsung, another sponsor, had no fewer than fifty-four buses promoting their Galaxy S3 mobile phone. Another of the First Bus Volvos departs from Stratford bus station on 29 July. Both the Visa and Samsung ads had all been removed by the end of the year.

The third major sponsor to have mass bus advertising was Vodaphone with forty-one buses promoting their 'Freebee' offer. Arriva's T53 is seen, not near Stratford but at Croydon beneath the wires of the Tramlink on 11 August. Some of these adverts would last into autumn 2013.

Coach Travel

Another element of the overall travel plan was the provision of coach services. These included services for athletes and spectators and 'park and ride' facilities at some venues (for example Wimbledon and Weymouth), in addition to private hire coaches. One of the challenges was providing suitable parking areas for coaches. Existing National Express coaches, commuter services and sightseeing services were also affected by road closures and stopping restrictions.

Air Travel

A temporary terminal was created at Heathrow Airport to be used by over 10,000 departing athletes after the Games.

River Thames Services

Existing riverboat services were enhanced during the London 2012 Games, with a number of piers utilised for spectators including Greenwich Pier, Woolwich Pier and Canary Wharf Pier.

During the London Olympic Games in 2012, some cruise ships were employed for the duration. German ship *Deutschland* was anchored in West India Dock where she was used as a hotel and for corporate hospitality by the German authorities. Here she was on 27 July. Built in 1998 and owned by Peter Deilmann Reederei, this and the *Berlin* have been regular visitors to the Thames.

Royal Navy assault ship L12 HMS *Ocean* was sited at Greenwich during the Olympic Games as part of the security against possible acts of terrorism. 5 August 2012.

Thames Clippers grew out of a peak-hours commuter ferry service between Canary Wharf and Embankment started by Collins River Enterprises in 1999. By 2012 their main service, RB1, ran from the London Eye to North Greenwich every twenty minutes off-peak with extensions to Woolwich Arsenal Pier at certain times. Their original vessel, the 1999-built *Storm Clipper*, here departs from Woolwich. During the Olympics they issued a *Games River Bus Timetable*.

Tower Bridge was adorned with a set of Olympic rings. On 8 July 2012 the west walkway was transformed into a 200-foot-long *Live Music Sculpture* by the British composer Samuel Bordoli. Thirty classical musicians were arranged along the length of the bridge 138 feet above the Thames behind the Olympic rings. The sound travelled backwards and forwards along the walkway, echoing the structure of the bridge. After the main Olympics the rings were replaced by the Paralympics emblem.

Walking and Cycling

Walking and cycling was also encouraged, with a 'Greenway' established between West Ham station and Stratford. This was a rebranding of the existing Sewer Bank, a pathway which covers the route of the Northern Outfall Sewer, built as part of Sir Joseph Bazalgette's original London sewer network. Strategic walking routes were identified to complement the London Cycle Network, with additional information and signage provided where appropriate.

A view from 2020 along the Greenway from near West Ham looking northwards. The roof of the Olympic Stadium is just visible in the distance.

One of the signs erected at entrances to the Greenway, which remains a popular walking and cycling route.

London Buses

Your guide to buses during the 2012 Games

Stratford

July – September 2012

MAYOR OF LONDON   Transport for London

The cover of a leaflet issued by London Buses during the Games which listed bus routes serving Stratford, along with a map of the area.

Information and Signage

TfL publicity before and during the Games included 'Gear up for the Games' aimed at the coach industry with maps of principal roads and locations of venues. A central London bus map and some local travel guides were printed. Information entitled 'Get Ahead of the Games' was also provided on the TfL website. Games guides handed out a season ticket folder with a 'Get Ahead of the Games' booklet inside.

Pink directional signs to Games venues were mounted at certain Underground, Overground and DLR stations. Smaller pink labels appeared on the maps and diagrams within trains. Signs on bus stops warned of road closures during the Games.

Amongst other publicity produced was a leaflet from Newham Council entitled *Walk 2012 Games, Stratford London* offering walks around the periphery of the Olympic Park.

Games Makers and Olympic Champions

The services of an army of volunteer guides in their distinctive uniforms, known as 'Games Makers', was seen as one of the big success stories in the smooth running of the Games. A target of up to 70,000 volunteers was set and there were over 240,000 applicants. Rail operators also provided Olympic Champions, who were based at key stations to provide information and advice and special training was provided. Additional security staff were also hired to manage crowd control and security at railway stations and venues.

Legacy

The Olympic Park Site

Part of the Olympic Park site became the Queen Elizabeth Olympic Park, the biggest new London park in over 100 years. There was much improvement to the existing riverbanks to improve accessibility and enhance the ecology. While part of the Channelsea River was culverted, the Waterworks River was widened. The Carpenters Road lock was reconstructed with new radial gates fitted in 2017. As well as functioning as a lock these gates can also be used to distribute water around the rivers for flood prevention. In May 2022 control of the Olympic Park transferred from the LDDC to the London Borough of Newham.

The Olympic Stadium (now renamed London Stadium) has become the new home for West Ham United football club. More than 9,000 new homes have been created in what has become the E20 postal district through new building and the adaption of the former Athletes' Village.

By the end of 2014 the Greater London Authority reported that London's population had grown to 8.6 million, an increase of 12 per cent since 2001. The fastest future growth was expected to be in Tower Hamlets and Newham, two of the Olympics host boroughs.

Most of the area once occupied by the Temple Mills wagon works, sidings and goods sheds has metamorphosed into East Village, with Westfield Stratford City to the south and Stratford International station between the two.

North-west of East Village a 'vibrant new community' called Chobham Manor has taken shape. Beyond that, Olympic facilities for cycling, hockey and tennis have been retained at the Lea Valley Hockey & Tennis Centre and the Velopark.

Development is ongoing within the former Olympic Park site, with new phases of construction bringing homes, jobs and cultural facilities to the area. The former Press and Media centre has become 'Here East', a business innovation centre. The International Quarter is also being developed as a business hub. This will be a home for organisations as diverse as the Financial Conduct Authority and the Nursing & Midwifery Council. A new university campus, UCL East, is being built to the south of the ArcelorMittal Orbit. This will cater for 4,000 students studying subjects as diverse as robotics and conservation.

A new creative centre will open at East Bank in 2022–23. A joint venture with University College London, London College of Fashion, the BBC, Sadlers Wells and the V&A, this 'will bring their expertise, resources and profile to deliver a new creative centre for artistic excellence, learning, research, innovation, performance and exhibitions and are already working with local organisations and partners ahead of the buildings opening in 2022/2023'.

No doubt, all this extra activity will bring additional passengers to Stratford, which has already become the busiest transport hub in Greater London and TfL will continue to develop rail and bus services to this area to meet the changing demands. The delayed opening of the Elizabeth line (Crossrail) in 2022 will be the first major development, opening up new direct connections to a part of London that has changed in character significantly since the 1980s, and particularly since the successful decision to bid for the Olympic Games to come to London in 2012.

The Olympic Stadium, now home to West Ham United and renamed the London Stadium. Originally built with a capacity of 80,000, it reopened in 2016 with a capacity of 66,000, limited to 60,000 for football matches. The removable seating design has also seen the stadium used for the 2017 IAAF World Championships, Rugby World Cup matches, and in June 2019 the first US Major League baseball game held in Europe.

The London Aquatics Centre, designed by Zaha Hadid, was one of the showpieces of the Olympic site. After the Games, the terraced wing seating on either side was removed and the present glass walls installed, with the centre reopening to the public in March 2014.

The London Aquatics Centre is by the side of the Waterworks River, one of several rivers running through the Olympic Park site. Boat trips are available.

Looking across the river towards the London Stadium and the ArcelorMittal Orbit. This 114.5-metre-high observation tower was designed by Sir Anish Kapoor and Cecil Balmond as a lasting statement piece. Since 2016 the world's tallest and longest tunnel slide (178 metres) has been added to attract more visitors to the site. The cranes to the left are at the construction site for the new UCL East campus.

While the Queen Elizabeth Olympic Park has the playgrounds, flower beds and the trappings you would expect to find in a park, the skyline shows the proximity of Westfield and the ongoing development of the area.

Westfield shopping centre seen from the pedestrian bridge over the station.

The main pedestrian route from Westfield to the London Stadium. Behind the hoardings, development of the East Bank site is progressing.

Above: One of the hoardings explaining the ongoing developments of the Olympic Park area.

Right: Another poster, informing of the development of the UCL East campus.

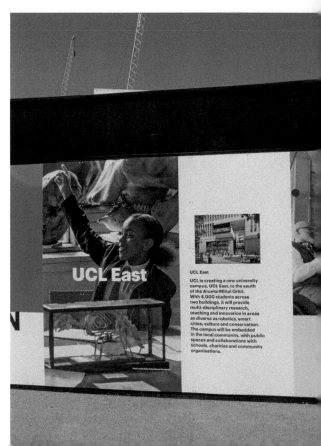

A view from the west in 2021 looking towards Stratford and showing existing and ongoing developments.

A view from the DLR Stratford platform 4 in September 2021 showing new development under construction to the west of the Westfield Marks & Spencer building.

2014 was designated in London as 'The Year of the Bus' with a number of special events. This included placing a number of these decorated 'New Routemasters' sculptures in various locations around central London, Croydon and the Queen Elizabeth Olympic Park. On 24–25 January 2015 the events culminated with all of these brought to the Olympic Park for display before being sold off for charity. Part of the display can be seen here.

A foretaste of the future perhaps? Public trials of this self-driving electric vehicle were undertaken in the Queen Elizabeth Olympic Park in September 2017. It was developed by French manufacturer Navya and operated by Keolis. It uses sensors, cameras and GPS mapping to navigate its route.

Railways

In the years after 2012 there have been a number of changes to the companies running National Rail franchises. The Greater Anglia local service between Liverpool Street and Shenfield transferred to TfL ownership as TfL Rail from 31 May 2015. This was in advance of it later being absorbed into Crossrail (Elizabeth line). The new Crossrail Class 345 EMUs began operating these services in June 2017. Initially these operated as seven-coach trains but following platform lengthening where possible they have now been lengthened to nine coaches ready for the opening of the full Elizabeth line service. The opening of the Elizabeth line between Paddington and Abbey Wood has been delayed several times since the original December 2018 opening date and is now expected to open in the first half of 2022. Services between Shenfield and Liverpool Street and between Reading/Heathrow and Paddington are expected to be connected to the initial Abbey Wood to Paddington section later in 2022.

Also, from 31 May 2015 local services from Liverpool Street to Chingford, Enfield and Cheshunt via Seven Sisters passed to London Overground. The c2c services franchise passed from National Express to Trenitalia in 2017. At weekends there are now regular c2c services from Liverpool Street calling at Stratford as well as their services from Fenchurch Street via West Ham. On the fringe of the area, the Barking–Gospel Oak line, which had passed from Silverlink to London Overground control in 2007, was electrified from 2016 with full electric services starting in 2019.

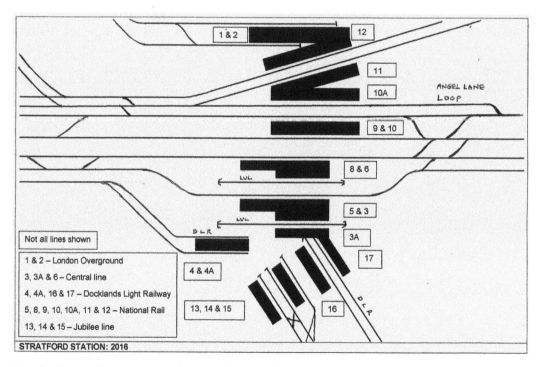

Stratford station layout in 2016. (Diagram by Jonathan James)

From 19 August 2016 the Night Tube services on Friday and Saturday nights commenced, initially running on the whole Victoria line and on the Central line from White City to either Loughton or Hainault via Newbury Park (and thus through Stratford).

Before Covid, Stratford was the busiest station on the Underground outside the Central Area Zone 1. However, in November 2021 the *Metro* newspaper reported that Stratford had overtaken Waterloo as Britain's busiest railway station, a title it had held for seventeen years. An estimated 14 million passengers travelled though Stratford in the year to 31 March according to the Office of Rail and Road (ORR.). They reported that other interchange stations such as Barking, Highbury & Islington and Clapham Junction were also in the top ten busiest stations replacing main London termini. Travel patterns had changed with a major decline in leisure travel during lockdown that had since recovered, while the influx of long-distance commuters has not recovered so much as people continue to work from home.

A view from platform 9 as a Freightliner train comes of the North London line and passes through Stratford in 2021. The ArcelorMittal Orbit can be seen as well as modern developments built since the Olympics. Contrast this with the view on page 11 taken from roughly the same viewpoint in 1985.

A view of the westernmost subway at Stratford in 2021 showing access to Stratford City and the Queen Elizabeth Olympic Park as well as to the other platforms.

Above: On Jubilee line platform 13 this plaque commemorates all the Team GB medal winners at the 2012 Olympic and Paralympic Games.

Left: Mounted at Stratford International station, this plaque commemorates the former railway depot that stood on the site beforehand.

With growing levels of traffic, Overground trains up to five coaches were proposed in the mayor's future transport spending plan statement of December 2012. Work started in December 2013 on lengthening platforms where possible with the Stratford–Richmond section expected to be completed between February 2014 and April 2015. Work was also undertaken to modify Willesden Depot and Silwood sidings were constructed between Surrey Quays and New Cross Gate to increase stabling capacity. As the extra coach was added to each train, this was prominently promoted on the front and rear of the trains as seen on No. 378204 at Stratford on 3 January 2016. (Photo by Jonathan James)

A 2021 view from Lea Junction as a London Overground train heads for Stratford. The complex of buildings around Westfield can be seen in the background while further development work is taking place to the right of the tracks.

Above: Lea Bridge station opened as Lea Bridge Road on 15 September 1840 and closed on 5 July 1985. In the final years there was just a residual peak-hours passenger service from Stratford to Tottenham Hale, via the one intermediate station at Lea Bridge (see page 13). A new station on the same site opened in May 2016. Costing some £11 million, it was funded with grants from Waltham Forest Council and legacy funding from the developers of Westfield. Initially there was a half-hourly service from Stratford to Tottenham Hale, seven days a week. From 7 September 2019 the service increased to every fifteen minutes from Stratford on Mondays–Fridays with alternate trains going through to Meridian Water or Bishops Stortford.

Left: Hackney Wick station was opened in 1980 as part of the reopening of North London line passenger services between Stratford and Dalston. During the Olympics it was one of the key stations being on the western periphery of the site, but due to potential overcrowding westbound trains did not stop at the station. In 2017–18 the station was modernised and enlarged. A subway between platforms now replaces the former footbridge.

Right: Many of the Southeastern Class 395 Javelin trains were given names of British Olympians noted for their speed exploits. This is No. 395001, named after double Olympic champion Dame Kelly Holmes.

Below: The next major development at Stratford will be when Crossrail (aka the Elizabeth line) services start, now hopefully in 2022. The new trains have been running on TfL Rail services to Shenfield since June 2017. Stations along the route have been upgraded to make them fully accessible as here at Manor Park where this new footbridge with lifts and stairs has been installed.

In order to make space for Crossrail to descend into tunnel, the DLR station at Pudding Mill Lane was closed, the tracks slewed and a new much larger station constructed on the new site in 2014.

Seen from the new Pudding Mill Lane station, the large concrete structure is the portal where the Crossrail tracks descend underground, on the site of the original DLR station.

Part of the former North Woolwich branch has been incorporated into the Crossrail route to Abbey Wood. Here at Custom House in 2020 the station has been rebuilt as there will be interchange with the DLR on the left. Much new high-rise building construction in the area is evident, contrasting with the single-storey houses on the right. The towers of Canary Wharf are in the distance. A bus on route 241 heads for Stratford City bus station.

Bus Services

Essex independent company TWH (Travel with Hunny) were quick off the mark with a daily route extension of their Harlow to Loughton service on to Stratford starting 1 October 2012 with route number E20 (as in the postal district). Unfortunately, the route only lasted until 17 November after problems with poor reliability and late running.

TfL were also quick to announce proposals for route changes to cover the road network that had been created within the former Olympic Park site. Some old road names like Carpenters Road and Waterden Road remained although the roads were now somewhat different to how they had been beforehand. New roads like Westfield Avenue and Celebration Avenue would gain a service as routes travelling to Stratford City bus station were amended to serve the new housing districts of East Village and Chobham Manor. Routes proposed for change in 2013 were the 97, 241, 308, 339, 388, D8 and new night route N205. The first development was a new temporary route 588 which started on 13 July from Stratford City to Hackney Wick via the new roads that had become available. Some of the other route changes began to be implemented from 31 August such as those to the 97 and 339. Routes 308 and 388 were extended on 14 December when the full length of Eastway became available and consequently route 588 was withdrawn from 15 December.

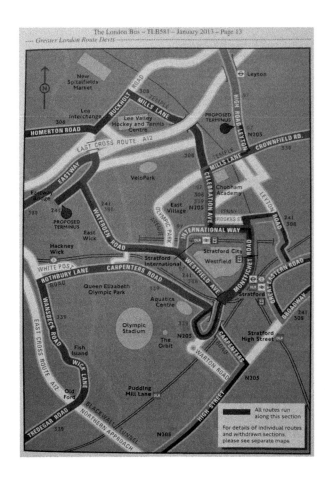

A map produced by TfL to accompany the route changes proposed in 2013 to serve new roads through the Olympic Park area. This was reproduced in the January 2013 edition of *The London Bus*.

On 9 April 3013 First Group announced that it was selling its London bus operations to two separate companies. The former CentreWest garages in West London were sold to Metroline who were the other main company in this area. The depots at Westbourne Park, Atlas Road, Willesden and Lea Interchange in East London went to a new player in the UK bus industry, the Australian-based Transit Systems Group, from 29 June. The new owners adopted the name Tower Transit. First's Dagenham depot's routes 193, 368, 498 and their vehicles passed to Go-Ahead in June who ran them from their Rainham garage. The other Dagenham routes 165, 179, 252 and 365 had all been won by Stagecoach on retendering.

Route changes were proposed to accompany the intended opening of Crossrail in 2018, mainly affecting links to the Crossrail station at Custom House. In the event the delay to Crossrail prevented these going ahead.

Lea Interchange garage in Temple Mills Lane was opened by First Group to replace their premises in Waterden Road. However, in 2013 First Group sold their London bus operations and this passed to a new company, the Australian-based Transit Systems Group trading as Tower Transit.

East London's Waterden Road garages were replaced by a new garage near West Ham station. This is seen at an open day held on 23 July 2016. On show were several of the latest types of electric and hybrid buses entering service in London at that time.

The opening of the Queen Elizabeth Olympic Park in 2013 prompted the extension or diversion of routes. Route 388 was one of these, being extended from Hackney Wick to Stratford City bus station. CT Plus HTL9 is in Westfield Avenue at the back of the shopping complex in November 2014.

In 2017, with new electric buses taking over the Red Arrow routes 507 and 521, some of the Mercedes-Benz Citaros previously used thereon were re-seated and transferred to work the 108 through Blackwall Tunnel. In this view MEC 9 has just departed from the Stratford International station terminus, to which it had now been extended. Behind can be seen some of the former Athletes' Village accommodation now turned into housing.

Another route that passes through the E20 postal district and serves Stratford City bus station is the 339 from Shadwell to Leytonstone. Tower Transit DM45120 is seen at the same location on the same day. This had been one of the four initial routes to serve Stratford City when it opened in September 2011 being extended from its then terminal at Bow, Fish Island, to the new bus station. It was extended to Leytonstone in 2013 and rerouted within the Olympic Park area during 2014.

From 4 March 2017 Tower Transit retained route 308 but converted it to double-deck operation. The route had started out originally with midi-buses but had been double-deck for the duration of the Olympic Games (see page 64). The new order saw it worked by these Volvo B5LH buses with MCV EvoSeti bodies. The route was rerouted in 2013 to serve the Chobham Manor area and Velopark and extended from Clapton Park (Millfields) to Clapton Lea Bridge Road roundabout where MV38242 is seen in 2021.

From 15 May 2017 Go-Ahead London's commercial division gained a new contract to provide a frequent link from Stratford City (for rail station) to Here East, a business and innovation park based in the former Olympic Press and Broadcast Centre. Three Wright StreetLites were initially used, and these carried dedicated vinyls in varying colours as with WS35 seen here with the Queen Elizabeth Olympic Park in the background.

Back-up for these was provided by a Dennis Dart, seen here heading out to Here East. The ArcelorMittal Orbit dominates the skyline.

New vehicles for CT Plus in 2016–17 were these stylish Alexander Dennis Enviro400H City buses. This is 2534 departing from Stratford City bus station on 1 September 2017. The route had been extended at its western end to Elephant & Castle.

Route 388 had been rerouted in 2013 via new roads through the Olympic Park and also passes the Here East business park. No. 2534 is seen again on Waterden Road.

A new venture from 4 June 2018 saw EOS launch express service S1 from Harlow to Stratford via the M11 motorway. Running Mondays–Fridays approximately every two hours it stopped at only Redbridge station and Stratford City bus station in London. On 29 June the 15.30 departure leaves Stratford and passes by the International Station on its way back to Harlow. The regular vehicle was ex-Go-Ahead London ED27 an MCV-bodied Alexander Dennis Enviro200 still in LT red livery. However, the route was withdrawn at the end of July without replacement.

With the limits on seating capacity imposed during the Covid lockdowns, the Streetlites on the Here East contract were replaced by larger vehicles. Mercedes-Benz Citaro MEC14 received the dedicated vinyls and is seen departing the stop opposite Stratford City bus station on 1 April 2021.

Other vehicles have also been employed at times including Alexander Dennis Trident EN3 in 'Commercial Services' livery seen at the same stop.

From late August 2021 spare BYD electric buses have been used on the contract – this is SEe42 approaching Stratford City on 6 September.

Stratford bus station still looks much as it did when opened in 1994 but note the new high-rise developments in the background.

Coach services to Stanstead Airport, etc., have been switched from picking up outside the south side of Stratford station to a stop opposite Stratford City bus station where this National Express coach has arrived in 2019. There are no longer through trains from Stratford to Stanstead – passengers can change at Tottenham Hale or travel direct from Liverpool Street.

Route 178 used to run from Maryland station to Clapton Pond via Hackney Wick until 1971. The low railway bridge in Carpenters Road, Stratford, necessitated low-bridge double-deckers with a sunken offset upper-deck gangway – the last of this type of bus in London. On 18 April 2021 there was a road run to commemorate fifty years since withdrawal. Preserved RLH61 travels along a part of Carpenters Road very different to when it last ran on the route. The road run could not exactly follow the old routing throughout – Carpenters Road was partially closed because of building developments and the clearance of the bridge has actually been reduced now.

Epping Ongar Railway

The single-line extension of the Central line from Epping to Ongar had closed after a protracted run-down on 30 September 1994. It had been the intention that the tracks would be left for a heritage group to take it over, but they were outbid by a property company, Pilot Developments, who offered to reinstate a commuter service and subsidise this by running wine and dine steam trains and 'Back in Time' experiences to be run by a paying franchisee. They bought two 1962 Stock Tube trains but the commuter service never materialised as London Underground would not let them run into Epping station. However, the Epping Ongar Railway Volunteer Society acquired a diesel multiple unit which ran at weekends between Ongar and North Weald (later extended to Coopersale) from 2004–07. The company, by now renamed Epping Ongar Railway, later bought some steam locomotives and carriages from Finland. However, as these were to a wider 5-foot gauge they would not run on the existing tracks. In 2008 there was a major bust-up among the directors when Roger Wright, latterly owner of Blue Triangle Buses, refused to back the other directors over their plans to re-gauge the line and run the Finnish locomotives. It came to a sealed-bid process for control and Roger Wright was able to use some of the profits from the sale of Blue Triangle to the Go-Ahead Group (see page 41) to make the winning bid and take sole ownership of the railway. It was then closed for four years from 2008–12 while it was thoroughly rebuilt and restocked, opening as a heritage steam- and diesel-operated railway on 25 May 2012. During the Olympic Games the railway ran daily, but now runs at weekends from Easter to October and certain other days during school holidays and the Christmas period.

The official press reopening was on 24 May 2012. The EOR's flagship locomotive, GWR Hall Class No. 4953 *Pitchford Hall*, breaks through the banner at North Weald to mark the official launch of services. Public services began the following day. (Photo by Rodger Green)

The Epping Ongar Railway is unique in running its own bus services. As trains are not able to work into Epping station where both platforms are used by LUL, on operating days, bus route 339 provides a link from Epping station to the railway at North Weald, with some journeys continuing to Ongar and (since 2014) Shenfield. The service is registered as a route so that local passengers can be carried as well. Former London Transport vehicles from the associated London Bus Company fleet are used. RT3062 waits outside Epping station on 26 May 2012, the second day of public reopening on the Epping Ongar Railway.

Bibliography

Batten, Malcolm, *East London Buses: The Twenty-first Century* (Stroud: Amberley, 2019)

Batten, Malcolm, *East London Railways: From Docklands to Crossrail* (Stroud: Amberley, 2020)

Carr, Ken, *Campaign: London's Advertising Buses 1969-2016* (Boreham: Visions International, 2016)

Glover, John, *London's Underground 12th Edition* (Addlestone: Ian Allan, 2015)

Glover, John, *Rails across London* (Manchester: Crecy, 2018)

Buses (Shepperton/Hersham: Ian Allan) monthly magazine

Modern Railways (Ian Allan/Key Publishing) monthly magazine

Docklands Light Railway: Preparing for the Olympics – special supplement in Tramways & Urban Transit (Hersham, Ian Allan, May 2006)

The London Bus (London, London Omnibus Traction Society) monthly magazine

Various other publications, including fleet lists published by the London Omnibus Traction Society. This is the principal society for enthusiasts of London Transport and its successors, and anyone with an interest in the London bus scene past and present is recommended to join. www.lots.org.uk